Now

Purposeful Steps Toward a More Abundant Life

Sarah Coller

Creaking Door Publishers
Bella Vista, Arkansas

Published by Creaking Door Publishers
Bella Vista, Arkansas

ISBN-13: 9780692811603
ISBN-10: 0692811605

Scripture quotations are taken from the New King James Version of the Bible, except where otherwise noted.

Creaking Door logo designed by Lynzie Coller
Digitalized by Kim Bourrie

Printed in the USA

Dedication

I was born into a lineage of strong and courageous women.
This work is dedicated to:

My Mother – The selfless and compassionate
Christy Lee,

My Grandmother – The creative and spirited
Betty Louise,

My Great-Grandmother – The brave prayer warrior
Irma Mae,

and to my daughter, the no-nonsense Lynzie Mae.
May you always greet life with arms wide open.

Right Now

One day a couple years ago, I was driving home from doing errands and mindlessly flipping through radio stations, when I had one of those moments I'll always remember. A spiritual experience, for sure.

I recognized Van Halen's, *Right Now*, and stopped to listen to this iconic song from my teen years. There have been a few times in my past when listening to Van Halen accompanied a spiritual experience, but since none of them were actually blessed by the *Holy Spirit* I'll just keep those to myself.

I'd been feeling frustrated with how I was living. No routine, little self-control, lots of wishy-washiness on important issues. I could sense that so many changes needed to happen but I was overwhelmed with trying to decide on a starting point.

So I was just driving along, hearing words that I've known by heart since I was 16 but had never really listened to; when all of a sudden God, in the form of Sammy Hagar, started shouting a little louder.

I parked in the driveway, sort of trance-like at that point. (That's the not the first time I've been trance-like during Van Halen either). I felt like something was jerking me upright and smacking my face into reality as the last line screamed at me.

Yeah. Totally in tears. Really, what *was* I waiting for? I've always been the type to want to have everything in place before jumping into something new. An organizer. A scheduler. But it was this day that I realized I was waiting for perfect circumstances while my *right now* was passing me by.

****

Do you have big goals that seem impossible because of your life circumstances? Are you ready to step out into fulfilling your dreams but everything seems so overwhelming?

My desire is to encourage you to take small steps toward those dreams *right now*---and to be satisfied with what you are able to accomplish *right now*. There's nothing more encouraging to move us forward in our goals than a feeling of positive progress. It's my prayer that you will begin to take joy in small strides that will eventually result in big successes!

Sometimes we hear the word, "abundance" and we want to equate it with prosperity. Abundance isn't necessarily the amount of things we acquire. It can be a state of being that we choose to live in. It can be a mindset that requires positivity and creativity---especially when we are *not* living in financial prosperity. In fact, financial prosperity can actually hinder the abundant life because it can make us less reliant on God and less likely to seek his perfect will.

There's no time limit on this study. You may choose to read the whole book through in one sitting and then go back to answer questions. Or, you might decide you'd like to take it slowly and pray through each section, seeing how the material applies to your unique situation. In any case, I pray this study blesses you and helps you live an abundant life---right where you are!

Pray and Respond

Think back to "a-ha" moments when you've made commitments to change or to start something new. List them here.

What life circumstances caused you to set these aside? These reasons don't have to be "good" reasons or even make sense right now. This is just an exercise to get you thinking.

What does it mean to you to live an abundant life?

Purging Procrastination

Years ago, a friend told me something that made a huge impact. She said, *"Perfectionism leads to procrastination."* This idea resonated within me as I wanted to perfect so many dimensions of my life. I wanted to be a godly wife and mother, a diligent homemaker, an encouraging friend, and a writer and speaker who would make an impact on her audience. I had developed aspirations regarding the best ways to reach my goals and was bent on accomplishing everything exactly how I'd imagined.

It wasn't long before I was feeling frustrated and wondering why I was failing---even with all my good intentions. Why couldn't I develop a daily quiet time like all the *real Christian moms?* Why couldn't I finish a craft project or a piece of writing? Why couldn't I take joy in any of my attempts to improve myself?

Soon, I began putting away my craft supplies. I hung up my creative writing hat and started writing social media marketing articles for any brand that would hire me. I stopped painting picture frames to match my furniture. I stopped making up artistic treats in the kitchen. More than that, I stopped reading my Bible as often as I had in the past. My well of creativity was running dry and I was avoiding the Living Water needed to fill it back up.

It sounds crazy now, but I convinced myself that if I couldn't spend time with God in the "right way" then he didn't want any of my measly efforts. I would read books and blogs about homemaking, homeschooling, and the Proverbs 31 woman and wonder why I just couldn't get it together. I would scroll through Pinterest and imagine all the amazing projects I was going to recreate...someday. In short, my doing stopped but my dreaming continued.

Feelings of insecurity about not doing something *perfectly* can cause us to avoid the work it takes to meet our goals. When we're faced with something as overwhelming as perfectionism, we tend to find distractions to fill our time and tell ourselves we'll refocus once we finish that one. last. thing.

Striving for Perfectionism Leads to Distracting Procrastination.

As God has mercifully continued to direct me, (even when I was not the most cooperative pupil) I've learned some skills and truths that would have made those years of questioning myself so much more fruitful. The purpose of this study is to help you take steps *now* to begin living your life to the fullest, *now.* I guarantee it's not going to look perfect at the beginning---but you know what? It's not going to look perfect *ever*. Break that perfectionist mentality and you'll accomplish good things, right from the start! Like my mom says, *today only comes once*. So I say, make it a day worth experiencing.

Pray and Respond

How have you let perfectionism distract you from your goals? Can you think of an instance when you wanted to move forward but the thought of messing up scared you into backing up?

In what ways have you stopped pursuing a dream or calling?

1 Corinthians 12 tells us our gifts are given to us by God for the profit of everyone. How is it an act of disobedience to God when we avoid using our gifts and talents because of feelings of fear or intimidation?

Do you have a specific goal in mind that you'd like to pursue? Write it below. You can give a lot of details pertaining to time limits or methods of achieving it---or you can write just a few simple words to identify it.

Jesus, Be the Center

Before making a plan of action, it's important to take a little time to make sure you've got a solid foundation on which to build. Ask yourself: is God my passion? Is he my driving desire? Will these new steps be steps of faith that will glorify God? He wants to inspire you and direct your path. More than that, he wants to partner with you in every endeavor.

God wants to partner with you in every endeavor.

When I was newly married and new to following God, he told me something during an early morning Bible study (back when I had quiet mornings available) that was foundational for me. He said, *"Make time for me and I'll make time for you."* He wasn't just saying he'd set aside time in his schedule. Instead, the message he spoke to me was that he would *create* time for me. If I'd put him first, he'd make sure all those other "important" things I had to do would work themselves out also. Unfortunately, I've not held up my end of that bargain very well. Still, I find that when I take the time to pray for wisdom and direction before stepping out into something new, things tend to go *much* more smoothly!

"To humans belong the plans of the heart,
but from the Lord comes the proper answer of the tongue.
All a person's ways seem pure to them,
but motives are weighed by the Lord.
Commit to the Lord whatever you do,
and he will establish your plans.
The Lord works out everything to its proper end—
even the wicked for a day of disaster."
Proverbs 16:1-4

<u>Pray and Respond</u>

What does it mean to you to make glorifying God your passion and driving desire?

How can the pursuit of your specific dreams glorify God?

How will partnering with God in the pursuit of your goals look different than going after them without his guidance?

In this space, journal your thoughts and note anything important the Lord has shown you.

The Heart Check

I've had the chance to know many women from many walks of life and one trend has really stood out to me. I call it the "Mid-30s Freakout." I don't know what it is about the 30s, but it seems to be an age when some women begin to experience restlessness and frustration about their life circumstances. Their realities aren't meeting their expectations and they begin searching for a change.

We all reach a point where we look at our lives and know there's something more out there. Oftentimes, we go looking for it in all the wrong places and end up hurting ourselves and others. On top of that, we receive no fulfillment and the damage we've created is sometimes irreparable. Several years ago, I saw myself heading for that place of looking for something more. My relationship with God was good but I had unfulfilled longings that seemed unexplainable. I began to think about what I was missing, personally. I love to learn, and I knew there was a huge world outside of my small town American culture, so I began to travel. (More on that later.) I've met interesting people from all over the world, have found lots of inspiration for writing, and have taken some pretty great selfies, to boot!

Why tame that free spirit when I can feed it in a way that meshes well with my life circumstances? I didn't need an entire life overhaul. I just needed to take steps toward a goal and toward living a full life right where I am.

When we pray for wisdom, we are giving God a chance to reveal to us our true hearts. It's always good to check your motives when you are looking for a change. Are you bored, frustrated, discouraged? These aren't necessarily wrong reasons for seeking something new, as long as what you're seeking is going to bring you into a closer walk with the Lord.

Are you feeling lonely or left out? Are you fighting with your spouse or kids and feeling dissatisfied with your life? Maybe you're thinking there's something more out there than what your own circumstances have to offer? Sometimes we women can feel restless and discontented and we feel like we need to escape. We become bitter and resentful that we have put aside goals and dreams for the, often monotonous, life of homemaking and motherhood. If you're feeling this way, know that you're not alone and it's very normal. More importantly, know that God has a better way of life ready for you to embrace. Escaping is not the answer and you likely don't need more "me time". What you may need, however, is a strategy for weaving your personal goals and dreams into the fabric of your current responsibilities and family life. It's important to take steps toward dream fulfillment without stepping on those you are charged to care for in the process.

If you are a person who finds yourself feeling that longing for something more, I encourage you to think about what it is that you're missing. Maybe it's Jesus. If you've got Jesus, then it's likely you need to take some time to figure out what else stirs your passion---then prayerfully pursue it!

When we pray for wisdom, we are giving God a chance to reveal to us our true hearts.

Pray and Respond

Describe a time (or times) when you dealt with unfulfilled longings. What made these desires unattainable at the time?

We often ascribe a negative connotation to the phrase, "free spirit". How do you feel about this term? How can a free spirit glorify God?

How can you harmonize your personal goals with those that you've made with your family or others to whom you're responsible?

Do you need to make changes in the discipline or routine of your children, your personal schedule, or other areas to allow yourself time to work toward your goals?

Looking for Change? Change Your Mindset

If there's one thing I want you to take away from this study, it's that so much about living an abundant and fulfilling life has to do with your mindset and *very little* has to do with your circumstances.

"And do not be conformed to this world, but be transformed by the renewing of your mind, that you may prove what is that good and acceptable and perfect will of God." Romans 12:2

No matter how big or small, your goals are important. Honor yourself by treating them as priorities on your list. It is always possible to make an improvement. All you need is to take one step forward.

You might be working on a goal to have your home "company ready" at any time of day, but the thought of getting into a housekeeping routine overwhelms you. (This was me for so many years, ladies!) Your one step might be as simple as committing to getting dressed each morning before doing anything else. This way, you can at least begin with meeting visitors on the porch! When you've succeeded at adopting this one good habit, it will be easier to wrap your mind around accomplishing even more.

Perhaps your goal is to grow all your own vegetables and herbs but you have absolutely no gardening experience. Your easy first step is to buy some seeds and stick them in a cup of dirt. Commit to watering it on a schedule. If you can water one seed on schedule, you can someday care for an entire garden on schedule. You're making a positive step forward and getting rid of that perfectionist mindset that keeps you trapped and immobile.

No matter how big or small, your goals are important.

What if we go a little deeper? It's ok, I won't put you on the spot. I'll talk about myself for this one.

Life's hard knocks often affect our minds and hearts in negative ways. Somewhere along the line, I began battling a tendency toward sarcasm and a critical spirit and I've always been a little leery about change. In grade school, I was one of the mean girls who picked on new kids just because they had come in and disrupted the order of my little world. Unfortunately, that kind of behavior translated into a judgmental spirit as I got older.

I found myself picking people out and making up little dialogues for them---things I thought they'd say or think---and judging their character with my critical spirit before I'd had the chance to get to know them. I *hated* this part of me!

One day, a big change was made within a ministry I was a part of and a new leader came in. Immediately, the biting, sarcastic thoughts began. I started mentally ticking off all the things about the person that would make it impossible for us to have a relationship. Then, I thought back on a woman I'd mentally done that to in the past--- only to find out she wasn't at all the difficult person I'd dreamed up. I didn't want to feel negativity like that about people anymore and I knew I needed a God intervention fast! I thought about all those "ask me" verses in the Bible where Jesus tells us to ask in His name and our prayers will be answered.

I stepped out against a critical spirit that morning and I prayed that God would help me to love the new leader fiercely. I even prayed these words: *"God, help me to see (the person) as you do and to love as you do."* Then, I went about my day and actually forgot about the situation all together.

That very evening, God brought the new leader to my mind. I found myself in tears, happy tears, over the way I felt about this person. In one day, God had taken bitter sarcasm and turned it into overwhelming love---all because I prayed! When you're praying God's heart, he doesn't mess around; but it all started with me choosing to take one prayerful step to change my mindset.

Pray and Respond

Thinking about the goals you listed previously, what are one or two simple steps you can take to start making them a reality?

I said, "No matter how big or small, your goals are important." What reaction do you have to that statement? Do you agree? Do you want to agree but something is holding you back?

It Doesn't Hurt to Ask

When I was a brand new wife 18 years ago, a woman came up to me after a church service and said she felt God leading her to share this verse with me:

"Ask, and it will be given to you; seek, and you will find; knock, and it will be opened to you." Matthew 7:7

At the time, we were pretty much living off cereal and sweet tea so I figured it was a sign that steak was in my future. In fact, I saw this verse as financial or material in nature for a really long time because for a really long time, I thought my biggest needs were financial. However, if you've done any real living at all, you know that money doesn't fix heart issues. God already promised in Matthew chapter six to take care of our physical needs. To live our lives to the fullest, sometimes we need to look beyond our physical circumstances and focus on what we're telling ourselves. Then, we need to ask God to change our *mindset*.

At a recent women's conference I attended, a speaker shared a message based on the story of the Samaritan woman found in the book of John, chapter four. When she got to verse 10, I was taken aback:

"Jesus answered and said to her, 'If you knew the gift of God, and who it is who says to you, 'Give me a drink,' you would have asked Him, and He would have given you living water.'" John 4:10

Wow. If I really understood who God is, I'd have no hesitations about asking him for the strength, wisdom, direction, time, and resources needed to live a fulfilling life.

There are a lot of those "ask me" verses in the Bible, but we're often confused about the way it all works. You say, "God, you said you'd give us whatever we ask for in your name (John 16:23). I've been praying to lose 50 pounds for a year now and you've done nothing for me!" We're missing the point of this whole deal. God will answer prayers *in accordance with his will*. How do we know his will? Well, we've got to read The Book.

Pray and Respond

Sometimes we need to look beyond our physical circumstances and focus on what we're telling ourselves. What have you been telling yourself about your personal dreams, goals, and callings?

Take some time to think about the questions you ask God. What are your hesitations about asking him for each of the following when it comes to living an abundant life?

<u>Strength:</u>

"Have you not known? Have you not heard? The everlasting God, the Lord, the Creator of the ends of the earth, neither faints nor is weary. His understanding is unsearchable. He gives power to the weak, and to those who have no might he increases strength. Even the youths shall faint and be weary, and the young men shall utterly fall, but those who wait on the Lord shall renew their strength; they shall mount up with wings like eagles, they shall run and not be weary, they shall walk and not faint." Isaiah 40:28-31

Wisdom:

"If any of you lacks wisdom, let him ask of God, who gives to all liberally and without reproach, and it will be given to him. But let him ask in faith, with no doubting, for he who doubts is like a wave of the sea driven and tossed by the wind." James 1:5-6

Direction:

"Thus says the Lord, your Redeemer, the Holy One of Israel: 'I am the Lord your God, Who teaches you to profit, Who leads you by the way you should go." Isaiah 48:17

"I will instruct you and teach you in the way you should go; I will guide you with My eye." Psalm 32:8

Time:

"But seek first the kingdom of God and His righteousness, and all these things shall be added to you." Matthew 6:33

"A man's heart plans his way, but the Lord directs his steps." Proverbs 16:9

Resources:

"You did not choose Me, but I chose you and appointed you that you should go and bear fruit, and that your fruit should remain, that whatever you ask the Father in My name He may give you." John 15:16

"And my God shall supply all your need according to His riches in glory by Christ Jesus. Now to our God and Father be glory forever and ever. Amen." Philippians 4:19-20

Should I Stay or Should I Go?

"See then that you walk circumspectly, not as fools but as wise, redeeming the time, because the days are evil. Therefore do not be unwise, but understand what the will of the Lord is." Ephesians 5:15-17

I once heard a pastor describe his decision-making process like this:

When making a decision, about 10% of the time I get an obvious red light. About 10% of the time I get an obvious green light. About 80% of the time, God says, 'Here are a few options. Pick one and I'll bless it.'

What a freeing thought! So many times, I wait for that audible voice from Heaven, coupled with the absolutely undoubtable *sign of confirmation*. Then I question the sign until I've completely explained it away and end up starting all over again. In most cases, I think we just have to step out in faith and look for his confirmation

31

(or red flags) along the way. This is how we function within our God-given free will and this is how we grow.

I've always needed an outlet for my desire and gifting to share my thoughts in writing. A few years after I left college and found myself missing the regular schedule of purposeful writing, I began blogging. At first, my blog was a place to unload random thoughts and ramblings and my only readers were friends and family. After awhile, I started building a following and my blog, coupled with my social media presence, became a thriving ministry. When I decided to expand that ministry to include publications, I questioned whether this was ok with God. I prayed and prayed for that elusive sign---but all I got was crickets.

One night it dawned on me: that ministry opportunity is here. It's right now. I'm doing it and it's blessing others. There are no red flags, there's no nudge in my spirit that says, "stop". God is blessing women as I'm faithful to encourage them with his truths; so as long as it's here before me, I'm just going to keep on doing it.

Sometimes we just have to step out in faith and look for God's confirmation along the way.

Are you passionate about something and you just can't let it go? For several years, I wrestled with guilt because the "writing a book thing" just kept coming up. I wondered if it was something that would distract me from my most important calling. My family has always been my first calling; and for a while, it was my only calling. As I began to mature and settle into a structured routine as a wife, mother, and homemaker, the doors began opening for me to function within the ministry God gave me for those outside my immediate family. The reason God continues to stir my passion for encouraging women is because he has a plan for me to encourage women. It's not a distraction--- it's a tap on the shoulder.

Unless you are completely fulfilling all God has for you in every way, you're likely feeling that tap on the shoulder, as well. So what are you waiting for? We're not promised tomorrow.

What is *the thing* for you? I want to encourage you to consider it, make sure it's going to count for eternal good, and then take a step toward making it a reality in your life. Sure, God might slam the door right in your face. Oh, but what if he opens it up wide and says, "Girl, come on in!"

This is why it's so important to train ourselves to hear the voice of God. It's not going to be an audible boom in a clap of thunder. It's going to be a nudge to our spirit through scripture, the confirming words of a Bible-believing friend, and the peace we feel when we've covered it in prayer and God says, *"Go forward in a way that honors me and I'll bless it."*

Pray and Respond

How has God given you confirmation or red flags about decisions in the past?

What passions nag at you and how have you tried explaining them away?

Do you feel confident you can recognize God's voice? How does he speak to you? If you're unsure, pray for discernment that you'd hear him more clearly.

It All Begins With a Step

There are a few particulars about my life that I'd like to change. I'd like to lose some weight, work on my attitude, and stick to a better housekeeping routine. Some people have bigger things like addictions or habitual sins that need a breakthrough. These are all things that we have the power to change, but we often want the changes to happen immediately, easily, and as painless as possible. If we can't see immediate results, we give up and stay where we are. There is a sense of safety in the familiar---even if the familiar is lukewarm, depressing, or even toxic. We often treat our dreams the same way and that's why they continue collecting dust on the shelf rather than becoming thriving realities in our lives.

When I started blogging eight years ago, one of the first blogs I read said something like the following: *"blogging is a nice start, but eventually you have to move past that if you want to be a successful writer."* Unfortunately, I allowed that line of thinking to discourage me before I'd even started.

Eight years of professional work as a blogger has proven those thoughts as bogus, but I couldn't see that on my first foray into the world of writing for the public. I saw that quote and immediately thought that what I'd just established---the baby step I had taken toward a career in writing---was not enough. Looking back, I realize how much I have learned. Blogging was essential to my growth as a writer and that time was a gift from God. Here are just a few ways I grew as a writer through blogging:

- I learned about networking and establishing friendships with other writers.
- I came to understand the various writing markets.
- I learned about e-publishing.
- I greatly expanded my worldview.
- I learned how to effectively communicate with those I disagree with.
- I became bolder in expressing myself and standing on my convictions.
- I learned about marketing and negotiating contracts.
- I practiced expressing myself succinctly.

Eight years ago, my life and family structure was not favorable for writing a book. I had five children under nine years old and was expecting a sixth. My husband was working full time during the day and taking college classes during the night. I didn't have the help, free time, or quiet moments that I have now that he's graduated and I've got a few teens to help me out. I could have chosen to keep that writing dream on the shelf because I wasn't able to make it look exactly like I wanted it to. Instead, I chose to take a smaller step and begin a blog. I had an outlet for my writing that soon turned into an excellent income and is now serving as a springboard for launching publications.

I'm getting closer to my big dream and while it's taken a lot longer than I'd have liked it to, there's not one of those smaller steps I'd trade in for immediate fulfillment. Each one of them served a good purpose to bring me to where I am today.

If I'm not willing to take the difficult first steps and do those menial things that are not as exciting as what my more experienced friends are doing, I need to rethink my goals. Being willing to lay the groundwork for my future shows maturity and dedication to my dream. If I will remember that *perfectionism leads to procrastination*, I can trust that even the tiniest of steps gets me closer to success.

Being willing to lay the groundwork for my future shows maturity and dedication to my dream.

Starting with small steps helps me see flaws in my logic and shows me how I need to adjust my plans. It gives me time to work something new into my routine because, as I've said before, my first calling is to my family and home. It's much better to make gradual changes than to jump in headfirst. The dream that has been built gradually has much more staying power than the whim I acted on without thinking it through well.

You may say, "first you're telling me to jump in because I'm not promised tomorrow and now you're telling me to go slow and don't rush it. What gives?"

While it may seem ironic that I'm talking about holding back in a book about going forward without delay, don't misunderstand. I'm not saying, *do nothing*---I'm saying, *don't skip steps*. This is why it's so important to start focusing on living your life to the fullest now because baby steps take time to complete.

"To everything there is a season, a time for every purpose under heaven." Ecclesiastes 3:1

Pray and Respond

Think of something from your past that you're proud of. Write down all the positive ways that experience helped form who you are today.

What baby steps have you already taken toward making your dreams realities?

What are some other preparatory actions you'll need to take?

In this space, journal your thoughts and note anything important the Lord has shown you.

Know Your Purpose and Beat Discouragement

So, you've decided it's time to test the waters and step out into something new. You've prayed about it and God has cracked a door open a little. You gently tiptoe your way up to it and hesitatingly press it open a few more inches with a shaking hand. All of a sudden, WHAM! You're met with a great big monster of opposition. It could be anything from a discouraging remark to a scheduling conflict, but you're bummed and feeling defeated. Congratulations, friend. You're probably on the right track.

Any time we decide to step out into a new venture, we're going to face some kind of pushback. Call it an attack of the enemy or just Murphy's Law---but whatever you call it, you need to be prepared for it. The best way that I've found to beat discouragement in any situation is to know my purpose.

You're probably familiar with the story of Queen Esther and her uncle's famous line:

"Who knows whether you have come to the kingdom for such a time as this?" Esther 4:14. Esther probably accomplished a bunch of stuff in her lifetime, but she's remembered for the act Mordecai was referencing in this verse---the deliverance of her people from the threat of genocide. She was a young woman, no different than you or I, but she knew her purpose and she didn't let fear, doubt, or discouragement keep her from fulfilling her calling.

It's not an accident that you and I were put on the Earth during this time in history. Just like Esther, we each have a unique role to play. The gifts, aptitudes, and abilities we were entrusted with as God skillfully knit us together in the wombs of our mothers are tools designed to bless others and bring them to Christ. That longing you have to learn the guitar or open a bakery or write a novel---who knows whether you have been put here with that desire for such a time as this? God doesn't play guessing games. If you're praying about something strongly weighing on your heart and you're getting nothing but open doors, take a step forward. If you're doing it to bless God and to be obedient, you can trust that he will be faithful to lead you into it or caution you from it.

"Trust in the Lord with all your heart, and lean not on your own understanding; In all your ways acknowledge Him, and He shall direct your paths." Proverbs 3:5-6

****

Like I said earlier, the majority of what it takes to live an abundant life has to do with mindset. It can be hard to convince ourselves that we are fit for the task of going after big dreams.

"But we all, with unveiled face, beholding as in a mirror the glory of the Lord, are being transformed into the same image from glory to glory, just as by the Spirit of the Lord." 2 Corinthians 3:18

In previous verses in 2 Corinthians chapter three, Paul talks about the glory of God shining on Moses' face. He had to wear a veil so the children of Israel could look at him---but this also covered the fact that the glory was passing away. Those who are in Christ have been "unveiled" and are able to be changed, "from glory to glory." We are living in the transformative light and freedom of Christ and He will equip us for every good work!

"Most assuredly, I say to you, he who believes in Me, the works that I do he will do also; and greater works than these he will do, because I go to My Father. And whatever you ask in My name, that I will do, that the Father may be glorified in the Son. If you ask anything in My name, I will do it." John 14:12-14

We read histories of great men like Moses who did mighty things for God and we feel ashamed or disappointed that we're not great like they were. We are forgetting about passages like John 14:12-14 that tell us we are able to do even greater things for God than Moses did. We can become more and more like the image of Christ as He grows us from one glory to another.

Have you been lied to by the enemy who wants to steal your confidence? Philippians 4:13 says, "I can do all things through Christ who strengthens me." Whatever we are facing, we can be sure that God will strengthen us to bear it courageously and confidently when we call on the name of Jesus!

Pray and Respond

How have fear and discouragement kept you from walking strongly and courageously in your calling?

List some pushbacks you've received after stepping out into something new. How did you deal with them?

Imagine yourself standing tall, shoulders back, taking a confident step toward your dream. Can you picture this? How does it make you feel?

The Comparison Trap

As I write these very words, I am sitting in a library study room, 20 minutes from home. Two hours ago, I was laying in bed with my napping daughter, playing Candy Crush Jelly Saga on my phone, and wishing I could be a real writer like my friend who had just arrived in South Carolina for a weekend writer's conference. I hadn't worked on this book or any of my own projects for months and was feeling pretty bummed. Then came the quiet voice: *the only thing stopping you is you.* Oh yeah, that's right. Silly me. A writer writes. She *writes.*

So, I got up and put my bag together, gave my oldest daughter dinner instructions and headed for the library. I've got a meeting in about an hour, but for now I'm writing.

Sister, stop comparing yourself to others. You've heard it a million times. I know you have because I read the same stuff you read and see the same stuff you see and live on the same planet you do and I *know.*

I'll never be my friend who is posting spa photos from South Carolina and prepping for a weekend of writing and speaking inspiration. (Although I think I'm gonna try to get in on that conference next year!) I was uniquely made and put where I am in God's historical timetable for a purpose only I can fulfill. (Even if I *do* have to do it with Arkansas-humid-curly-freakout hair and frazzled mommy brain.) Spending my time wishing I were there instead of here is going to serve one purpose---to distract me from what I'm supposed to be doing *here*.

Don't waste time comparing yourself to others. Accept your strengths as much as your weaknesses and grow in them both. Because, you know what? *Not all weaknesses were given as obstacles to overcome.* In most cases, God will use those very weaknesses as a testimony of his grace as you walk through life holding your head up in confidence and in his strength. He'll use them to make you authentic and approachable. *The bigger the fumble, the bigger the humble,* right? Humility teaches us to be compassionate to others.

∗∗∗∗∗∗∗∗∗∗∗

There are a zillion clichés regarding the fear of failure. "You've got to sink before you can swim", "You'll never know if you don't try", and the list goes on. They can be super annoying---but they're true. If we're ever going to conquer the scary, there has to come a point when we take a step *into* the scary.

When I was 33 years old, I had an epiphany. I was getting older. To make matters worse, I wasn't getting any younger. Ever.

46

I have a friend who hosts annual tours of England in association with her sewing pattern company and I've been on her announcement list for a long time. I always look forward to seeing her email come in the late winter of each year, announcing the upcoming itinerary. For several years, I would receive her email and dream about the neat places and activities she and her tour participants were going to experience. I'd never been further than 500 miles from my hometown, had never flown, and had only visited three states. In the past, it had never really bothered me---but the year I was 33, it did.

Suddenly it became really important to me to stop making decisions based on fear. I had been avoiding many opportunities to grow because I was afraid of failing, nervous about the reactions of others to my choices, or scared of all the dangerously bad stuff that could happen to me.

I wanted to take that England trip for so many reasons, but mostly to prove to myself that I could.

I remember the way I felt after I talked to my husband and got his blessing. His "yes" wasn't a permissive yes as much as an, "I believe in you" sort of yes. It was at that point I realized I had been looking for someone to confirm I was capable of traveling to this far away place, navigating airports, trains, and tubes, and wandering around unfamiliar cities on my own. I just needed a little encouraging push and my husband provided it for me. In fact, I think he and God have a conspiracy against me as they continue to nudge me into the uncomfortable places where they know I will blossom.

This book is the result of one of those loving pushes and that's why you're reading these words today!

A younger me wouldn't admit it, but there are times when I need someone just to say, "Yes, I believe in you. You can do this." Sometimes I want to show my independence and say I don't need anyone's permission to do "the thing". That's true, I don't. However, I *do* need the encouragement and prayer support of friends---and a little wise counsel never hurt anyone.

Pray and Respond

Do you have a tendency to get caught in the comparison trap? How has this stifled progress in the past?

Have you avoided doing "the thing" out of fear? I mentioned three fears: the fear of failure, worrying about others' reactions, and the fear of unexpected affects. Are these fears you deal with? Are there others? Write about them below.

Who do you have in your life that can give you an encouraging nudge out of your comfort zone and help you take your first steps?

"Listen to advice and accept instruction, that you may gain wisdom in the future. Many are the plans in the mind of a man, but it is the purpose of the Lord that will stand." Proverbs 19:20-21 ESV

Allow for Speed Bumps, Potholes, and Head-On Collisions

Warning: Life doesn't go according to plan. Prepare for failure.

Well that's a little discouraging! But it's also reality.

I was recently visiting with a newly married friend who, along with her husband, was going through a disappointing life change. They were frustrated, angry, disappointed, and a little scared. I did my best to encourage her, explaining that the struggles they were facing were the normal stuff of life. Most strong and successful people have experienced conflict along the way. In fact, many successful people deal with difficult times despite their wealth or fame. The stuff of life is not a respecter of persons.

Our goal should not be to avoid life's disappointments; instead, we need to learn how to manage them while keeping our hope in tact. Once we have the right attitude about the struggles life throws our way, we can peer through the haze of disappointment and see the beautiful places God desires to take us.

When life isn't going according to our plans, we should recognize that it might actually be going according to *God's* plan. Further, I believe that if I make a habit of praying for God's wisdom and continual direction to be present in my decision-making, I have nothing to fear when I'm side-swiped by the unexpected. I'm learning to be still and wait on the Lord during hard times because it's in those times he teaches me about his nature and goodness. It's in those trials I see his provision and I realize where the miracles that see me through are coming from.

"I will lift up my eyes to the hills—
From whence comes my help?
My help comes from the Lord,
Who made heaven and earth.

He will not allow your foot to be moved;
He who keeps you will not slumber.
Behold, He who keeps Israel
Shall neither slumber nor sleep.

The Lord is your keeper;
The Lord is your shade at your right hand.
The sun shall not strike you by day,
Nor the moon by night.

The Lord shall preserve you from all evil;
He shall preserve your soul.
The Lord shall preserve your going out and your coming in
From this time forth, and even forevermore." Psalm 121

On a road filled with speed bumps, potholes, and head-on collisions, God might be leading you into something better than you've imagined. As long as you've handed over that steering wheel, you don't need to fear where he's taking you.

****

My kids and I have this joke that it's always the first day of school at our house because I'm really bad about sticking to the schooling schedules I write up. Even with lots of planning and the best of intentions, we are just not a five-days-a-week, nine-months-a-year kind of homeschooling family. We each have diverse goals and I'm a sucker for giving the kids lots of time to explore their own interests. That said, my kids *do* need an appropriate education and Jamie and I have committed to taking on that responsibility entirely. I know the kind of homeschooling mom I am, so I often need to implement back up plans B, C, and D to make sure we get on track after a distraction. Otherwise, setbacks can pile up and put the kids far behind where I'd like them to be academically.

When we recognize that frustrations and setbacks are a normal part of life, we can prepare for them well. Whenever you're stepping out into something new, it's a good idea to anticipate potential scenarios in which you may find yourself dealing with unfortunate complications.

This might sound counterproductive, but it's always wise to have a way *out* of the place your goals will take you---just in case you find yourself in over your head!

This is why I encouraged you earlier to start small and build on your plans a little at a time. Say you've got a goal to open a gift shop stocked with your own handmade items but you've saved no money to begin. Rather than taking out a huge loan and setting up shop next week, maybe start with an Etsy shop or a vendor booth at a local flea market. This way you can confirm there is a sufficient demand for your items and you can save a little money back for breaking out on your own. This will also help you make sure you enjoy crafting items on a time crunch and see if that kind of mass production is realistic for the time you have to spend.

Sometimes our holdups aren't huge hurdles to overcome, but just the simple responsibilities we've taken on that may need a little adjusting. For instance, when I decided I wanted to devote more time to writing professionally, I knew I was going to have to make some lifestyle changes if I wanted to keep a peaceful atmosphere within my home. With 11 people sharing a modest-sized house, it's difficult to find a quiet place to think and write. Our children are involved in several activities outside the home so my husband and I adopted a rhythm for taxiing them around. I take responsibility for the daytime happenings and he does most of the evening and weekend events. This gives me a quiet home a couple nights a week to work on my writing projects uninterrupted. I've also adjusted our homeschool schedule to allow me a nap in the afternoon. This way I can stay up later in the evenings to write when everyone else is sleeping.

It's important to discuss your goals with those to whom you're responsible so they can work with you on a compromise to free up more time or resources. I've read "self-help" sites that insist you be *proactive* and *demand* what's needed to fulfill your dreams. They say no one will take you seriously if you don't take yourself seriously and that you must make your own way. I don't believe this to be true, in most cases. Those who love us want us to succeed, we only need to communicate our needs to them and be willing to experiment with some compromises of responsibility to find the best rhythm for our own situations.

Some of life's hindrances to success, like lack of time, money, or resources, can be avoided with some preplanning and communication. Others, like the loss of a job or health issues, are going to pop up regardless of the preparations we make. It's important to put our goals in the proper perspective when the stuff of life creeps in. Often, we can find a workaround that allows us to keep up a measure of momentum. Still, we are sometimes required to set our dreams aside *for a time* to handle more important issues.

When this happens, we are often blindsided and become discouraged. We see it as a failure and decide to give up. You've heard it said that you're never a failure until you stop trying. This is true so if you find yourself in a season of needing to set goals aside, look at it as a temporary bump in the road, rather than the death of a dream.

There are hindrances you can avoid and those you can't help. Don't assume every stumbling block is a sign from God to stop moving forward. God often allows us to experience difficulties to show us what we're made of and to draw us into a closer reliance on him.

Pray and Respond

How have your failures defined you in the past?

What tools can you implement to keep yourself from giving up when things don't go as planned?

What are some potential setbacks that would keep you from moving forward in your current plans?

How can you adjust or let go of some current responsibilities to allow yourself needed time and resources?

In this space, journal your thoughts and note anything important the Lord has shown you.

Going Forward

Now that you've had some time to define your goals and work through some of the obstacles that have held you back in the past, it's time to form a strategy for making these dreams become actualities.

Earlier in the book, I talked about taking one first step. There are several positive disciplines to adopt that will help you move forward.

Speak Truth, Speak Life

"Anxiety in the heart of man causes depression, but a good word makes it glad." Proverbs 12:25

When Jamie and I were newly married, a popular new marriage book was sweeping churches and Bible study groups by storm: *The Five Love Languages* by Gary D. Chapman. In it, Chapman describes different ways that men and women feel loved by others. He offers a test allowing the reader to see how she and her husband best receive love. The idea is that the actions that make you feel loved are often the same things you will do to show love to others; but if you're not speaking the other person's love language, they won't understand your acts of love and won't receive it as you'd hoped.

I bring that up because when I first took Chapman's test at 19 or 20 years old, I learned my love languages were acts of service and quality time. At that point in my life, we were just starting our family and life had changed for me a lot. From my perspective, I needed help and I needed a break. If I were to take that test now, I bet my top love language would be words of affirmation. Using my marriage as an example, I know my husband loves me because he *shows* me every day. He's been a kind and encouraging husband with a servant's heart for over 18 years. However, lately I find that I'm asking his opinion much more often than normal. I'm attempting to draw him into long conversations (and trying really hard to stop to let him speak so they're not totally one-sided!) I'm finding that I need to hear words from him---encouraging words that I can hold on to when I'm having a difficult day. Just last night he sent me a Facebook message from church and said he was proud of me. In an instant, so much crazy from the day was overshadowed by that one kind truth that he took the time to "speak" to me.

"Pleasant words are like a honeycomb; sweetness to the soul and health to the bones." Proverbs 16:24

It's amazing how words spoken out loud can really change an atmosphere, that's why we should be careful to say things that are true and positive and life-giving. Do you ever give yourself a pep talk? We can turn our negative

60

days around by revitalizing ourselves with affirming words. Learn some encouraging scriptures and speak or sing them during difficult times. It's almost impossible for discouraging thoughts to overtake your mind when you're busy recalling the words to an uplifting worship song.

Don't forget the most important and guaranteed source of encouraging truth and life-filled words: our Heavenly Father. When we stop to pray in the midst of an overwhelming day, we feel God speaking peace and rest. We feel his encouraging words and they strengthen us.

Words spoken out loud can change an atmosphere. Speak things that are positive and true.

Pray and Respond

What positive words can you speak out loud to give yourself hope and confidence?

Circle Your Wagons

One of the smartest decisions I've made was the commitment to being choosey about who I allow into my inner circle. With all my home and family responsibilities in this season of life, as well as my commitment to go forward with personal goals, I have just a tiny bit of time I can carve out for friends. Not only that, but I also have a limited amount of emotional energy to give to friendships. Even the best relationships are going to experience drama from time to time, so I have to be careful to not take on the emotional struggles of others. My young family needs me to focus inward on our own family dynamic more than outward on others' personal issues. I'm sure it won't always be like this, but for now I've got to be super frugal about that time and make sure I'm spending it well.

It's so important to surround yourself with friends who will respect your time and your unique family dynamic, rather than manipulate or pull guilt trips when you've got to change plans to accommodate something more important. As an adult, you deserve mature friendships---so go after them and don't settle. Like I tell my kids, there's a difference between a friendly acquaintance and a true heart friend. I've had just a handful of true heart friends, but that doesn't mean I don't value each of my many casual friendships.

When you're choosing heart friends to share your goals with, be sure to open up to the ones who are going to lift you up in prayer and encouragement. In addition, choose the ones who can be honest in a respectful manner. Friends who know us well can often pick up on issues in our lives that we're blind to ourselves. Confide in friends you can trust and do your best to be that kind of friend, as well.

Pray and Respond

Are you more inclined to share all your business with anyone who will listen? Or do you tend to keep things very private, only opening up to a handful of people closest to you?

Are you a fixer? Have the personal struggles of others affected your own emotions to the point of distracting you? Being honest, how many of these struggles were yours to worry about?

When those within our circles of acquaintance are going through hard times, we should *always* be willing to pray and provide solutions when we can. However, *emotionally* taking on the burden they're carrying can be detrimental to what God requires in our own lives. Remember that God desires to carry these burdens so be sure to leave them at his feet, leaving you emotionally strong to do his good work.

Learn to Say No

The older I get the more I realize that I really *don't* have to be on anybody's schedule but my own. Sure, I've got lots of responsibilities, but my time is my own to fill however I choose. No matter your situation, this is also true for you. We're all given the same number of hours to spend each day.

A few years ago, I decided I was going to live a no-obligation life. That doesn't mean I let go of everything and just flew by the seat of my skirt in a selfishly flamboyant whirlwind of narcissism. I just stopped saying yes to the stuff I actually wanted to say no to. Then I stopped feeling guilty about that.

Oh, the doors that were opened up to me! I started enjoying being a mother because I was doing it my way instead of the way my Facebook friend was doing it. I started seeing the beauty and uniqueness of my own marriage because I had the time to work on my attitude and actions. What's more, I *found myself* (to coin a super cheesy 80s-sounding term). Of course I still gave time to my family and home, but I also gave time to myself. Time to write, read, dream, create, imagine, travel, and explore. Time to stop trying to reinvent myself and instead, to embrace all that is me.

Pray and Respond

I mentioned a "no obligation life." What does that mean to you?

Do you find yourself being guilted into things you don't want to do? Do you guilt *yourself* into things you don't want to do?

What are some ways you put unnecessary guilt on yourself?

Be honest with yourself: are you really as indispensible as you make yourself out to be? There are certain roles we were tailor-made to fill, others that just need to be filled by someone willing, and still others that could probably be abolished and the ministry would be better for it.

Sometimes we spend way too much time trying to figure out if we're in the right ministry and wondering if we should take on that one. more. thing. Anyone with ears let her hear: just because it's good to do, doesn't mean it's good for *you* to do.

Assess Your Resources

When thinking about the essentials required to make your goals happen, it's good to start small; especially if what you're working toward is going to require some financial investment. Look around and see what you have that could temporarily meet your needs as you get a feel for where these new plans are taking you. You may be able to fill a lot of your prerequisites by being creative.

For instance, one of my wild dreams is to someday own a dusty, musty used bookstore. I want to specialize in old and rare books and offer tea and baked treats in a reading room decorated with Victorian antiques. Since I'll have kids at home for at least another 15 years, this is one of those future goals that I'm not focusing on too much right now. Still, it doesn't hurt to begin slowly working toward it, so I'm always on the lookout for free and super cheap books. I put a notice out to friends to let me know if they have books to donate that would otherwise go to a second hand store and I scour the markdown table every time I hit our library's book sale shop. When I get the chance, I list these books on eBay or Etsy; otherwise, I just set them aside for the future.

There have been many times that I've been able to get creative to meet the next step of my goals, and just as many times that I've prayed for provision and God has come through! Earlier this year, I wanted to set up a reading and writing nook in my dining room and told God I wished I had the furniture to do so. A week or so later, a friend called and said she had connections to someone giving away a couch and two armchairs. Of course I jumped on the opportunity and began setting up my room. I remember thinking I should be on the lookout for a little lamp to put in there so I could be up while the kids were sleeping without disturbing them. Before I got around to mentioning that to my family or even to God, my husband and kids surprised me with a super cute lamp for Mother's Day. They said they'd been walking through the store and just felt like they should buy me one. God looks out for us in big and small ways and often likes to make these seemingly insignificant things happen just to show us how much he loves us.

Pray and Respond

Make a list of the resources you will need to get started on the first steps of your goal. How many needs can you fill today? This week? Next payday? How many can wait for later?

Make a Plan to Turn Dreams Into Priorities

My family loves to tease me about my obsessive tendencies regarding schedules. I've always been pretty strict about meal and bed times; and the phrase, "sorry, you didn't put it on the calendar," gets me off the hook quite a bit. In my opinion, everything runs better on a schedule. I'm definitely the queen of organizational systems and even if most of them don't get implemented exactly how I'd hoped, the smallest amount of planning and prep still gives me a great start.

One of the best things you can do when you're moving from a place of dreaming about a goal to a place of implementing it is to make a schedule and put yourself on it. If you have to cancel plans with yourself, immediately reschedule.

Writing this book has been the best step toward my goal of becoming an author who writes daily and publishes multiple works each year. The deeper I get into the project, the more I've had to prioritize my time. There came a turning point when I realized I'm actually authoring a book. No longer was I just making notes for future projects. I reached a point of no return where I had to decide whether or not I was ready to take the next step. A step that required more of my time and less excuses.

I began scheduling blocks of time to write and edit. I found that I had to stop leaving home to find a quiet place to write and just press on through the noise and distractions. I had to stop looking for perfect circumstances and just do the next thing to the best of my ability. I had to keep those appointments with myself, even if I had to stop countless times to answer kids' questions, help with math, rotate laundry, make lunch, or lock the door and ~~beg God for mercy~~ pray.

"So teach us to number our days, that we may gain a heart of wisdom." Psalm 90:12

Pray and Respond

What do you do when your plans require you to cancel plans with yourself? Do you use this as an excuse to procrastinate?

If you feel you are ready, take out your calendar right now and make an appointment with yourself. Give yourself enough time to complete something productive toward your goal.

Obedience: Our Primary Motivation

My ministry to you through this study would not be complete if I didn't mention the most important aspect of living an abundant life: obedience.

Earlier in the book, I encouraged you to ask yourself: is God my passion? Is he my driving desire? Will these new steps be steps of faith that will glorify God?

He wants to inspire us and direct our paths, but following those paths requires our willingness to listen to his leading and submit. Too many times we want the blessings of success but our difficulties with obedience get in the way.

As a parent, I sometimes give my children instructions with no further explanation. I expect obedience. Out of trust, (and probably a little fear) they obey. As they've gotten older, they've often thanked me for steering them the right way, because they can look back and see that I was working for good in their lives.

I try to remember this concept when it comes to the things of God. We've heard the saying, "God's ways are not our own." Some Biblical concepts are beyond our comprehension, others just require an understanding of the Bible as a living and complete work. Still others are very clear, but seem difficult for us to apply to our own lives in a culture that doesn't comply with Biblical standards.

In each season of our lives, we'll be faced with opportunities to choose to obey God's directions to us. I think true peace comes when we pursue his higher ways and walk in obedience---even when it doesn't make sense.

Pray and Respond

In regard to this study, I encourage you to spend some time answering these questions about obedience:

How does God feel about my goals?

Are these goals going to bring me closer to him or distance me from him? How?

Do these goals interfere with responsibilities and callings that I know God has established in my life? If not, how will they compliment or enhance what I'm already doing in obedience to him?

In this space, journal your thoughts and note anything important the Lord has shown you.

Dear Reader,

I feel so blessed to have had the opportunity to speak into your life and I hope you've been inspired to take those small strides that lead to big successes. Don't let your *right now* pass you by!

If you would like to be notified of future publications, need information on speaking engagements, or would just like to chat, visit ClassicalHomemaking.com or email me at sarah@classicalhomemaking.com.

Blessings,
Sarah

Acknowledgements

As with any time-consuming work, this one was made possible only because of the encouragement and patience of those who care about me. Special thanks to my Arkansas friends, my Oklahoma girls, and everyone back in the Pacific Northwest for cheering me on via Facebook. It's been fun sharing my writing successes and editing freakouts with you all!

The relationships I've made with my online friends are very dear to me. Thank you to everyone, worldwide, who has read my blogs and followed me on social media the last eight years. You've been a great source of encouragement and inspiration.

To my children: Lynzie, Michael, Elisha, Cainan, Selah, Avalon, Liam, Kynthia, and Brenna; thank you for the patience, grace, and excitement you've shown during this project. Thank you for the housework, meals, and babysitting you've sometimes been responsible for. You are the joys of my life.

Finally, my husband Jamie. From the day I met you at 13 years old, you've modeled the character of Christ. This made me want to know Him, too! I will never forget the day you played Steven Curtis Chapman's, *You Are a Treasure* for me when I was 16 years old. Jesus sees beyond outward appearances and messy lives. You chose to, as well, and the two of you have been conspiring ever since to give me a beautiful life. Thank you.

About the Author

Sarah Coller is just a regular girl saved from her sins by the Lord Jesus Christ. Married since 1998 to her high school sweetheart and mother to nine sweet blessings, she stays busy homemaking and homeschooling. Her passion is to create a comfortable and peaceful home for her family.

In her free time, she also enjoys reading classic novels, shopping at flea markets, sipping tea, scribbling her thoughts, traveling, and enjoying all things British.

Sarah blogs at ClassicalHomemaking.com; and at her literature blog, BellesLibrary.com.

About Creaking Door Publishers

The beloved English author, Jane Austen, wrote much of her best work at a tiny writing table in the parlor of her family's cottage in Chawton, Hampshire.

Since it was considered scandalous in her day for a woman to publish under her own name, and because this kindred spirit of mine liked to keep her business to herself, Jane shared her writing with very few people.

She appreciated the "creaking parlor door" that separated that room from the rest of the family's home because it alerted her when someone was coming. She could then hide her work under a stack of papers and pretend to be writing a letter instead.

As a woman usually desperate to find a private place to write, I can relate to Jane's plight and have sometimes wished for an alarm system, as well. Perhaps one day I'll have a creaking door of my own installed in my home!

44989782R00048

Made in the USA
San Bernardino, CA
28 January 2017